TEACHING PROTECTIVE BEHAVIOURS
TO YOUNG CHILDREN

First Steps to Safety programme

Carolyn Gelenter, Nadine Prescott and Belinda Riley

Routledge
Taylor & Francis Group

LONDON AND NEW YORK

First published 2014 by Speechmark Publishing Ltd.

Published 2017 by Routledge
2 Park Square, Milton Park, Abingdon, Oxon OX14 4RN
711 Third Avenue, New York, NY 10017, USA

Routledge is an imprint of the Taylor & Francis Group, an informa business

British Library Cataloguing in Publication Data

A catalogue record for this book is available from the British Library

ISBN: 9780863889820 (pbk)

Contents

About the authors

Carolyn Gelenter trained as an early years teacher in Sydney in the early 1980s. After completing her studies, she worked in long day care for children aged 0–5 years. She then gained employment with Community Child Care Co-op in Sydney, at the time an advocacy and training organisation for children's services. Carolyn moved to the UK in the early 1990s and has worked across primary and special needs in London. Working in both inner-city Sydney and London led her to want to understand and work more effectively with children with language needs. As a result, she completed a postgraduate certificate in Speech and Language Difficulties from Birmingham University in early 2000 and then went on to do an MSc in Joint Professional Practice at City University and the Institute of Education. She has worked for Westminster Local Authority since 1999 in various capacities and as an advisory teacher for SLCN (Speech, Language, Communication Needs) since 2004. In 2010, the advisory service was transferred to Westminster Special Schools, where she is now based.

Nadine Prescott has worked as a Speech and Language Therapist for the past 11 years. She trained in New Zealand and started her career working in an urban rural mixed setting in the South Island of New Zealand. She moved to the UK in 2006 where she stayed for 7 years. She began her UK career working in inner-city London mainstream primary schools and then took on the role of Principal Speech and Language Therapist for the Speech & Language Therapy Service to Mainstream Secondary Schools in Westminster. Currently Nadine works for the Ministry of Education in Christchurch, New Zealand where she works with children aged birth to 21 years with a range of communication needs. She has worked across a range of different settings, including early childhood centres, nurseries, kindergartens, rural play groups, clinics, children's homes and mainstream primary and secondary schools. Nadine's work as a speech and language therapist has always had a strong focus on collaboration with others and she enjoys being part of projects involving other professionals and parents. She especially enjoys working with secondary school-aged students as they can be a large part of this collaboration by contributing to their therapy targets and intervention.

Belinda Riley is an experienced trainer and qualified social worker who has over 14 years' experience specialising in Child Protection and Safeguarding within Children and Families. She has extensive experience providing expert advice around safeguarding and child protection to a range of professionals within the Children's workforce. Belinda is originally from Perth in Western Australia but moved to London in 2002 where she continued her social work career.

Through Belinda's consultancy work across a number of London Local Authorities, in particular as a Child Protection (CP) Advisor and CP Case Conference Chair, she recognised the need for specialist safeguarding and child protection training and as a result has designed, developed and implemented a number of bespoke training programmes, in particular within the Education sector. It was through this work that Belinda recognised that there was limited education for children around safety awareness.

In 2012, Belinda completed the Protective Behaviours Foundation Course through Protective Behaviours UK.

About the CD

Teachers and other adults running the programme should refer to the enclosed CD for colour versions of the resources.

CD materials can be found at http://resourcecentre.routledge.com/books/9780863889820

Researching the maltreatment of children

There is a lot of research and evidence about how children are at risk of harm or abuse. This research indicates that abuse and neglect are both under-reported and under-recorded:

Approximately 46,700 children in the UK are known to be at risk of abuse right now.

One in four young adults (25.3%) was severely maltreated during childhood.

In 2009, the NSPCC did a major piece of research to give us a more up-to-date picture of child maltreatment. The NSPCC interviewed young people aged 11–24 years. The full research findings were published in *Child Abuse and Neglect in the UK Today* (Radford et al., 2011) and below some key findings from the summary report are listed.

Maltreatment of 18–24 year olds

- One in four young adults (25.3%) had been severely maltreated during childhood.

- One in seven young adults (14.5%) had been severely maltreated by a parent or guardian during childhood.

- One in nine young adults (11.5%) had experienced severe physical violence during childhood at the hands of an adult.

- One in nine young adults (11.3%) had experienced contact sexual abuse during childhood.

- Almost one in ten young adults (9%) had been severely neglected by parents or guardians during childhood.

(Based on a survey of 1761 young adults aged 18–24 years.)

Maltreatment of 11–17 year olds

- About one in five children (18.6%) have been severely maltreated.

- More than one in eight children (13.4%) have experienced severe maltreatment by a parent or guardian.

- One in 14 children (6.9%) have experienced severe physical violence at the hands of an adult.

- One in 20 children (4.8%) have experienced contact sexual abuse.

- One in 10 children (9.8%) have experienced severe neglect.

(Based on a survey of 2275 children aged 11–17 years.)

In another study, disabled children were found to be over three times more likely to be abused or neglected than non-disabled children (Sullivan and Knutson, 2000).

Definitions of child maltreatment used in research

Contact sexual abuse is defined as any sexual activity (such as touching and penetration) where (a) the activity is forced or coerced, (b) the child is under 16 and the act involves an adult over 18 or (c) the child is under 18 and the act involves a parent or guardian or person in a position of trust (as defined by the Sexual Offences Act 2003). It does not include sexual activity between young people aged under 18, if the acts are not forced or coerced.

Severe maltreatment includes physical violence, emotional abuse, neglect and contact sexual abuse. Abuse was classified as severe depending on: who the perpetrator was; how often it happened; if there was more than one type of abuse; if it resulted in a physical injury; if a weapon had been used; if it placed the child at risk of harm; or if it was defined by the victim as abuse.

Severe neglect includes emotional neglect or lack of physical care or supervision that would place a child at risk.

Verbal aggression is defined as: being embarrassed or humiliated, being shouted or screamed at, sworn at, called stupid or lazy, threatened with smacking or threatened with being sent away.

Introduction

First Steps to Safety incorporates 'Protective Behaviours', an abuse prevention programme which originated in the USA in 1978. Protective Behaviours focuses on two main themes: '**We all have the right to feel safe all the time**' and '**There is nothing so awful or small that we can't talk about it with someone**'. This edition of the programme aims to provide children aged 4–7 years with awareness and strategies for keeping safe. The information and strategies provided to children are generic and applicable across a range of situations that may arise; for example, bullying, internet safety, being harmed, feeling sad or feeling unsafe.

Through a mutual recognition that current programmes for teaching children safety awareness (i.e. 'stranger danger') are contrary to the evidence about who is placing our children at risk, this programme has been collaboratively developed by an advisory teacher, a social worker and a speech and language therapist. The abuse of children is rarely by a stranger; rather, it is perpetrated by someone known to them, including parents, carers, friends, extended family members, teachers and other people within their network.

Although it may be difficult to accept, children and young people from any community, including those with disabilities, can be put at risk of harm, abused or hurt, regardless of their age, gender, religion or ethnicity. All children have the right to be safeguarded from abuse or neglect so that they have the opportunity to reach their potential and be successful adults. Sadly, not all children are safe and many children and young people experience some form of abuse, neglect or bullying during their lives.

The First Steps to Safety programme

Protective Behaviours teaches children to develop an awareness of personal safety; helps them to identify and express their feelings; and helps them to make choices and solve problems. In First Steps to Safety we have taken the core protective behaviour principles and created a teaching framework with overarching aims, supporting lesson plans, resources and activities in a 10-week programme which can be picked up and used by anyone in a school wanting to empower children and young people of any age and any capability to develop personal safety.

Although this is a 10-week programme, the skills and lessons learned can be embedded in school culture and everyday practice in the classroom. The programme will also support you to evidence your safeguarding responsibilities under the OFSTED inspection framework.

While traditional protective behaviour programmes aim to be inclusive for all children, there is an issue of access for children with significant communication and learning needs. This programme aims to provide children with varying communication abilities the tools to communicate about their safety in a variety of ways. The focus is very much on preventive early intervention work for all children, including accessibility for vulnerable children.

The maltreatment of children can have major long-term effects on all aspects of their health, development and wellbeing and can have a deep impact on the child's self-image and self-esteem, and on his or her future. This is why it is important to develop an early intervention tool which focuses on prevention rather than cure. This is the aim of First Steps to Safety.

Members of staff using this programme need to be prepared to be open in discussion about bodies and using specific vocabulary. Normalising and openly discussing the genital area in an appropriate way and in appropriate settings will mean children will be more comfortable to talk about this too.

Aims and objectives

Overall aims

- To empower children to feel safe and know they have a right to feel safe.
- To give children the confidence and ability to assertively manage their own safety.
- To give children the skills to take responsibility for their own bodies, thoughts, feelings and behaviour.
- To enable children with a range of communication abilities to ask for help.

Objectives

At the end of this programme, children should:

- have a better awareness of their body, thoughts, feelings and behaviour
- have the vocabulary to express how their thoughts and feelings affect their bodies
- know the early warning signs for feeling unsafe
- know they can make different behaviour choices based on feelings
- know who good people are to go to for help ('my people network')
- know how to ask 'my people network' for help.

Routledge
Taylor & Francis Group

This page may be photocopied for instructional use only. *First Steps to Safety programme*
© Carolyn Gelenter, Nadine Prescott and Belinda Riley 2014

Session 1:

Getting started with First Steps to Safety

Introduction to Session 1
Getting started with First Steps to Safety

This first session introduces the children to the routine the sessions will follow and the resources which will be used consistently throughout each session. This session also gives time for children to develop a set of agreements, or ground rules, which will apply for all the sessions in First Steps to Safety.

This introductory session also introduces the two main themes of protective behaviours:

'We all have the right to feel safe all of the time'

'There is nothing so awful or small that we can't talk about it with someone'

While it is not envisaged that children will raise issues of concern at this stage, it is possible that, as the sessions develop, a child may reveal a safeguarding concern at some point during the programme. It is very important to establish an atmosphere where children feel safe to participate and raise issues in a safe and trusting environment. Therefore, this first session is about laying down the foundations for building relationships of trust between the children and the adults involved.

As this First Steps programme is geared towards young children, it is intended that the children learn as much as possible through the use of games and activities that they can relate their own experiences to. In addition, games can make learning fun and accessible if everyone sticks to the agreements that have been established by the class.

Session 1: *Getting started with First Steps to Safety*

Session objectives

- I will know why we are doing First Steps to Safety.
- I will know what the class agreement is.
- I will understand why I need to do what the agreement says.

Key words

agreement, first steps to safety

Session plan

Activity	Instructions	Resources
What are we doing?	<ul><li>Put up relevant cards so children can easily see them.</li><li>Go through the timetable with children so they know what will be happening to them during the session.</li><li>Take down each card at the completion of each activity.</li></ul>	'What are we doing?' cards
Starting song	<ul><li>Sing 'The Hokey Cokey' song.</li></ul>	Songs pack
Key words	<ul><li>Write the key words on the board for the children to see.</li><li>Get the children to say the words out loud with you and choose one of the following brief activities to help reinforce the new words.<ul><li>Break up the word into syllables.</li><li>Say the first sound of the word.</li><li>Put the word into a sentence.</li><li>Practise explaining what the word means.</li></ul></li></ul>	

Routledge
Taylor & Francis Group

9

Activity	Instructions	Resources

Introduce the two main themes	• Tell the children that we are going to be learning about keeping ourselves safe and there are two important things to remember.
	• Show the children the themes poster which displays these phrases:
	   • **We all have the right to feel safe all of the time**
	   • **There is nothing so awful or small that we can't talk about it with someone**
	• Get the children to say the phrases out loud with you.
	• These themes will be used at the start of each session and underpin all of the aims and objectives of this programme.
		Themes poster

Why are we doing this?	• Go through the points on the 'Why are we doing this?' poster. • Ask children if they have any questions.	'Why are we doing this?' poster 1
Make agreement	• Ask the children to think up four or five rules that they will agree to follow in the group (e.g. listen to each other, be kind, take turns to talk). • Write the rules on the agreement template and get all children to write their name on it to say they agree. Refer to this as an agreement. • Put the agreement up where all children can see it. • Show the children the reward chart. Explain that all children can earn points for following the agreement. If children achieve 10 points all together as a group, they can choose a fun game to play at the end.	Agreement template and reward chart
Play 'Hide the Teddy'	• Explain to the children that it is important we learn to help each other and work together to create a safe and happy classroom. • Explain the rules using the handout in the games pack.	Games pack

Activity	Instructions	Resources
Play 'Monsters'	• Tell the children they are going to play a game, which is a little bit scary as they will have to stop the monster from getting them! • Explain the rules using the handout in the games pack.	Games pack
Compliment circle	• Tell the children they have played a game where they all had to work together to find the teddy and one where they tried to scare each other! • Now it is important to feel safe again so we are going to choose someone we thought was really good at following the agreements and tell them what they did well. • Explain to the children that this is called a compliment.	Games pack
End of lesson certificate	• Children complete the end of lesson certificate as a summary of what they have learnt today.	End of lesson certificate
Finishing activity as reward	• Refer to the reward chart and agreement. If the children have received 10 points, they can choose a game or song to finish with (e.g. repeat a game or song from the lesson or choose from the games or songs pack).	Games and songs packs

Everyday links to this session

• Put the themes poster up on the classroom wall and refer to it again during the week.

• Make the compliment circle a regular part of your routine.

• Refer to the agreements throughout the week, not just for the session.

• Read stories about listening and getting along with others (see the recommended reading list).

• Play games where the children have to work together to help each other (see the games pack).

Session 1: Resources

Why are we doing this session?

Session 1

This session will help us to...

- Know what we are going to be learning about.

- Agree about our behaviour for the lessons.

Session 2:

My body parts

Introduction to Session 2
My body parts

As in Session 1, the children will follow a routine that includes reviewing their agreement, learning about what they are doing in the session, understanding why they are doing it, playing lots of games and doing other fun activities to help them learn about their body parts.

When introducing the idea of teaching young children how to stay safe, it is imperative to give them the language to express themselves in situations that may occur where they may feel or be physically unsafe. Children need the vocabulary to name body parts as well as to describe emotional states of being in order to communicate information about themselves and their needs. This includes learning the body parts that describe what are often called 'private parts'.

The authors of this programme believe that it is essential to teach children words that describe all parts of their body if we are really concerned with helping children to stay safe. We believe that talking about vaginas and penises in the same way as we talk about elbows and knees will help children develop a sense of their own bodies as something they have a right to feel safe about, rather than feeling embarrassed about. If we don't teach children to use these correct words as part of everyday life, how can we expect them to be able to communicate when something feels uncomfortable, unsafe or wrong to them?

Session 2: *My body parts*

Session objectives

- I will be able to name my body parts.
- I will be able to name the different body parts for girls and boys.
- I will be able to name my private body parts.

Key words

body, private parts

Session plan

Activity	Instructions	Resources
What are we doing?	• Put up relevant timetable cards so the children can easily see them. • Go through the timetable with the children so they know what will be happening to them during the session. • Take down each card at the completion of each activity.	'What are we doing?' cards
Agreement	• Revise the agreement and the importance of following it. • Put the agreement up where all children can see it.	Agreement template and reward chart

The two main themes	• Remind the children that we are going to be learning about keeping ourselves safe and there are two important things to remember.
	• Show the children the themes poster which displays these phrases:
	  ◦ **We all have the right to feel safe all of the time**
	  ◦ **There is nothing so awful or small that we can't talk about it with someone**
	• Get the children to say the phrases out loud with you.
		Themes poster

Routledge
Taylor & Francis Group

Activity	Instructions	Resources
Why are we doing this?	• Go through the points on the 'Why are we doing this?' poster. • Ask children if they have any questions.	'Why are we doing this?' poster 2

Key words	• Write the key words on the board for the children to see.
	• Get the children to say the words out loud with you and choose one of the following brief activities to help reinforce the new words.
	  ◦ Break up the word into syllables.
	  ◦ Say the first sound of the word.
	  ◦ Put the word into a sentence.
	  ◦ Practise explaining what the word means.	

Starting activity	• Sing the 'Head and Shoulders, Knees and Toes' song.	Songs pack
Main activity	**Body parts poster** • Explain to the children that their bodies are very special and it is important that they look after them, keep them clean and safe. • Explain that everyone has some similar body parts, but there are also some differences between boys and girls; and these are often described as private parts. • Ask children if they know the name of their private parts and why these are called private parts. (It is important to ensure that children know the correct names of the penis and vagina and why these are called private parts. You will need to be very encouraging as this is bound to create laughter and shyness.) • Explain to the children that you are going to play a game where they will place body part pictures on the outline of a body.	Large sheet of paper on which to draw body outline Body part pictures Small bean bag

Activity	Instructions	Resources
Main activity *(continued)*	• Divide the body part pieces among the children and ask them to put their piece on the body outline. When they place it, they have to say the name of the body part. • Once all the pieces are on the body, congratulate the children for doing so well. • Now that the children have the full pictures in front of them, explain that everyone is going to have a chance to practise saying the names. • Use a bean bag and get the children to take turns throwing it onto the bodies, naming the part of the body where the bean bag lands – give lots of praise when they name it correctly.	
End of lesson certificate	• Children complete the end of lesson certificate as a summary of what they have learnt today.	End of lesson certificate
Finishing activity as reward	• Refer to the reward chart and agreement. If the children have received 10 points, they can choose a game or song to finish with (e.g. repeat a game or song from the lesson or choose from the games or songs pack).	Games and songs packs

Everyday links to this session

• Continue to refer to the themes poster and get the children to keep repeating the two phrases.

• Put the body part pictures on the classroom wall.

• Sing 'Head and Shoulders, Knees and Toes' again.

• Find an opportunity during the week to reinforce the names of body parts.

Session 2: Resources

Why are we doing this session?

Session 2

This session will help us to...

- Name our body parts.

- Name different body parts for boys and girls.

- Name our private body parts.

Face

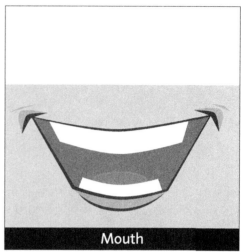

Mouth

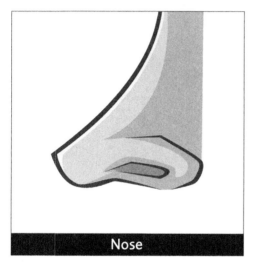

Nose

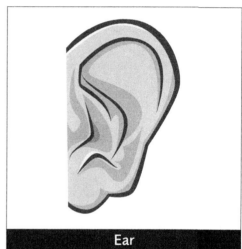

Ear

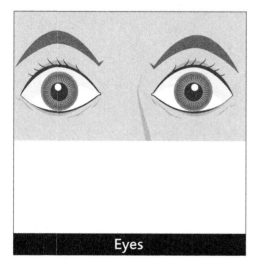

Eyes

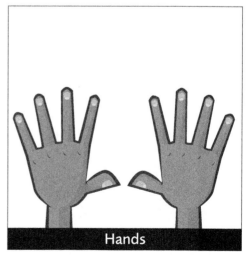

Hands

 Routledge
Taylor & Francis Group

This page may be photocopied for instructional use only. *First Steps to Safety programme*
© Carolyn Gelenter, Nadine Prescott and Belinda Riley 2014

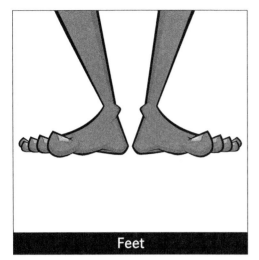

Feet

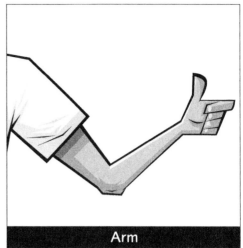

Arm

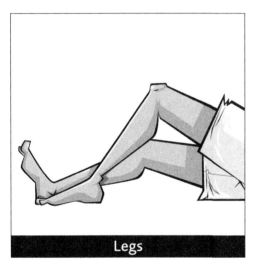

Legs

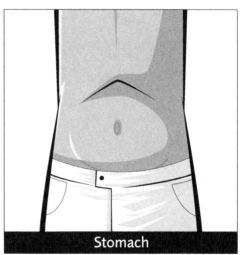

Stomach

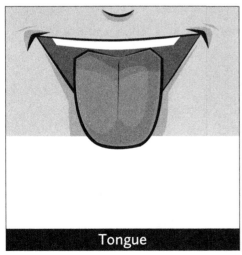

Tongue

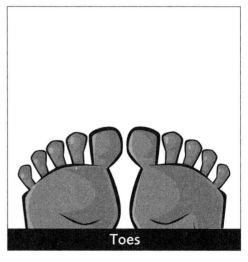

Toes

Routledge
Taylor & Francis Group

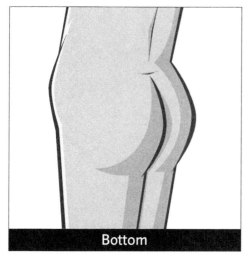

Bottom

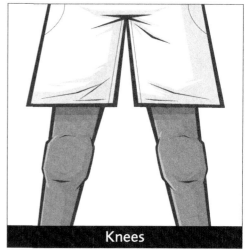

Knees

Head

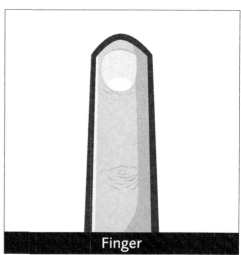

Finger

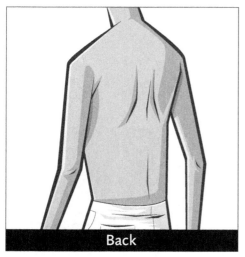

Back

Nail

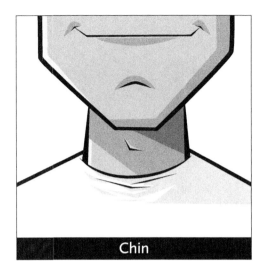

Chin

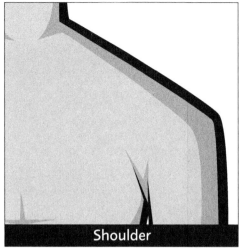

Shoulder

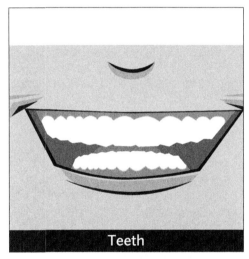

Teeth

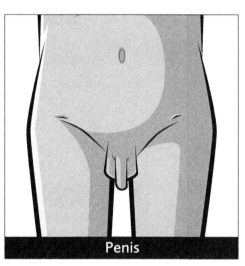

Penis

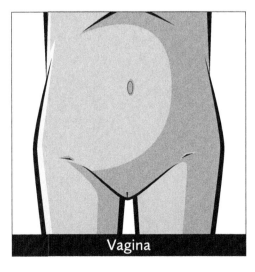

Vagina

Routledge
Taylor & Francis Group

Session 3:

Feelings are feelings

Introduction to Session 3
Feelings are feelings

This session focuses on one of the key principles of the protective behaviours programme – 'We all have the right to feel safe all of the time'. The activities and games in this session are designed to concretely reinforce that statement at a level that is developmentally appropriate for young children.

The children will understand that everyone experiences a range of feelings, that different experiences make us feel differently, and that our bodies and faces reveal how we are feeling. The children will have an opportunity to do activities and discuss how they might feel in everyday common situations that they may experience, such as getting into trouble with an adult or coming first in a race.

As in the previous sessions, the children will review their agreement and follow the routine. Once again, there are lots of games and activities, songs and stories that will both ensure the material is geared towards the children's developmental understanding and make the learning more active and fun where appropriate.

Session 3: *Feelings are feelings*

Session objectives
- I will be able to describe my feelings.
- I will be able to name good feelings and bad feelings.
- I will understand that we can have many feelings.

Key words
feelings, happy, sad, angry, excited, scared, surprised, bored, hurt

Session plan

Activity	Instructions	Resources
What are we doing?	• Put up relevant timetable cards so the children can easily see them. • Go through the timetable with the children so they know what will be happening to them during the session. • Take down each card at the completion of each activity.	'What are we doing?' cards
Agreement	• Revise the agreement and the importance of following it. • Put the agreement up where all children can see it.	Agreement template and reward chart

The two main themes	• Show the children the themes poster which displays these phrases:
	  • **We all have the right to feel safe all of the time**
	  • **There is nothing so awful or small that we can't talk about it with someone**
	• Get the children to say the phrases out loud with you.
		Themes poster

Activity	Instructions	Resources
Review	• Review the body parts activity from previous week. • Look at the bodies from last week. • Cover up the names of various parts of the body and ask different children whether they can remember what they are called. • Remind children that some parts of the body are private because it is up to them who can see and touch them in those places.	Body parts completed poster
Why are we doing this?	• Go through the points on the 'Why are we doing this?' poster. • Ask the children if they have any questions.	'Why are we doing this?' poster 3

Key words	• Write the key words on the board for the children to see.
	• Get the children to say the words out loud with you and choose one of the following brief activities to help reinforce the new words.
	  ◦ Break up the word into syllables.
	  ◦ Say the first sound of the word.
	  ◦ Put the word into a sentence.
	  ◦ Practise explaining what the word means.	

Starting activity	• Play the 'Pass the smile' game.	Games pack
Main activity 1	**Feelings** • Explain to the children that everyone has lots of different feelings and they can change during the day. • Sometimes we have happy feelings and sometimes we have sad feelings. There are no right or wrong feelings. • Put the sun and cloud poster up. • Show the children the different feelings cards and make sure they can label them.	Sun and cloud pictures Feelings cards

Activity	Instructions	Resources
Main activity 1 (*continued*)	• Get the children to say whether the card should be placed under the sun or the cloud. • Explain that one of the ways we can show how we are feeling is by the look or expression on our face. • Point to a feelings card and ask the children to show that feeling on their face.	Sun and cloud pictures Feelings cards
Main activity 2	**Our faces can show how we are feeling** • Give the children the blank faces worksheet. • See the instructions on the worksheet. Read out each situation to the children to make sure they understand them.	Blank faces worksheet and instructions
End of lesson certificate	• Children complete the end of lesson certificate as a summary of what they have learnt today.	End of lesson certificate
Finishing activity as reward	• Refer to the reward chart and agreement. If the children have received 10 points, they can choose a game or song to finish with (e.g. repeat a game or song from the lesson or choose from the games or songs pack).	Games and songs packs

Everyday links to this session

• Continue to refer to the themes poster throughout the week.

• Play the 'Pass the smile' game again.

• When praising children for good work, or reminding them about appropriate behaviour, use this as an opportunity to talk about feelings.

• If possible, have a life-like doll in the classroom role-play corner.

Session 3: Resources

Why are we doing this session?

Session 3

This session will help us to...

- Know how to name our feelings.

- Know we have lots of different feelings, some good and some bad.

33

Our faces can show how we feel

Draw how your face would look when you:
- Open a birthday present
- Play with your friends
- Get in trouble with an adult
- Have hurt your knee

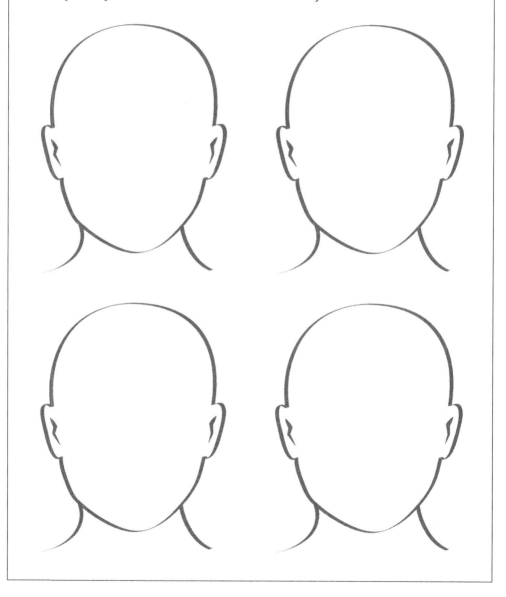

Session 4:

Showing my feelings

Introduction to Session 4
Showing my feelings

As feelings are such abstract and to some extent individual experiences, the authors think the children need more than one session to learn about feelings, as well as how they are related to thoughts and expressed in our bodies. This session therefore pursues the theme of feelings and looks at how sometimes we try to hide them. This is quite an abstract concept for children and, even at this young age, they may have learned strategies for hiding how they really feel.

This is an important session for linking the idea that our bodies can register feelings and our faces and bodies can show how we feel or allow us to hide our feelings as well.

It is important for children to understand that all feelings are acceptable but that how they behave may not be. This session is important in getting children to understand that it is important to talk about feelings rather than using our bodies to hide them or to hurt other people's feelings.

Session 4: *Showing my feelings*

Session objectives

- I will understand that I can show my feelings in different ways.
- I will understand that sometimes it is hard to talk about how I am really feeling.

Key words

showing feelings, hiding feelings

Session plan

Activity	Instructions	Resources
What are we doing?	• Put up relevant timetable cards so the children can easily see them. • Go through the timetable with the children so they know what will be happening to them during the session. • Take down each card at the completion of each activity.	'What are we doing?' cards
Agreement	• Revise the agreement and the importance of following it. • Put the agreement up where all children can see it.	Agreement template and reward chart

The two main themes	• Show the children the themes poster which displays these phrases:
	  • **We all have the right to feel safe all of the time**
	  • **There is nothing so awful or small that we can't talk about it with someone**
	• Get the children to say the phrases out loud with you.
		Themes poster

Review	• Refer back to the sun and cloud pictures and again sort different feelings under each one.	Sun and cloud pictures

Activity	Instructions	Resources
Why are we doing this?	• Go through the points on the 'Why are we doing this?' poster. • Ask the children if they have any questions.	'Why are we doing this?' poster 4

Key words	• Write the key words on the board for the children to see.
	• Get the children to say the words out loud with you and choose one of the following brief activities to help reinforce the new words.
	  ◦ Break up the word into syllables.
	  ◦ Say the first sound of the word.
	  ◦ Put the word into a sentence.
	  ◦ Practise explaining what the word means.	

Starting activity	**How do we show our feelings?** • Get the children to stand up. • Show the children the pictures of people showing different feelings. • Get the children to name the feeling they see in the person and to act out the feeling themselves, thinking about how their body and face will need to look.	Feelings cards

Main activity	**Hiding our feelings**
	• Read the book *Not Now, Bernard* to the children or alternatively watch and listen to the book online at www.youtube.com/watch?v=a2CjdRWmfdo
	• Do a Think, Pair, Share activity with each of these questions:
	  ◦ How did Bernard feel in the story when no one would listen to him or play with him?
	  ◦ What happened when Bernard did not talk about his feelings?
		'Think, Pair, Share' cards
		
		Computer screen to show YouTube clip or copy of book

Activity	Instructions	Resources
Main activity (continued)	• Do you think Bernard was really eaten by the monster, or do you think he really turned into a monster? • Emphasise that Bernard didn't talk about how he felt about not being listened to and so he felt so angry he turned into a monster! • Ask the children to think about a time when they could not talk about their feelings. What did they do? • Finish by explaining that we need to talk about our feelings to help us feel better. Say that we will be learning more about talking about feelings.	
End of lesson certificate	• Children complete the end of lesson certificate as a summary of what they have learnt today.	End of lesson certificate
Finishing activity as reward	• Refer to the reward chart and agreement. If the children have received 10 points, they can choose a game or song to finish with (e.g. repeat a game or song from the lesson or choose from the games or songs pack).	Games and songs packs

Everyday links to this session

• Give the children opportunities to talk about how they feel in situations that arise in the classroom or playground.

• Read or watch *Not Now, Bernard* again.

• Reread the story of *Not Now, Bernard*, inserting the children's names instead.

• Focus throughout the week on this phrase from the themes poster: **We all have the right to feel safe all the time.**

Session 4: Resources

Why are we doing this session?

Session 4

This session will help us to...

- Understand that we show our feelings in different ways.

- Know it can be hard to talk about feelings.

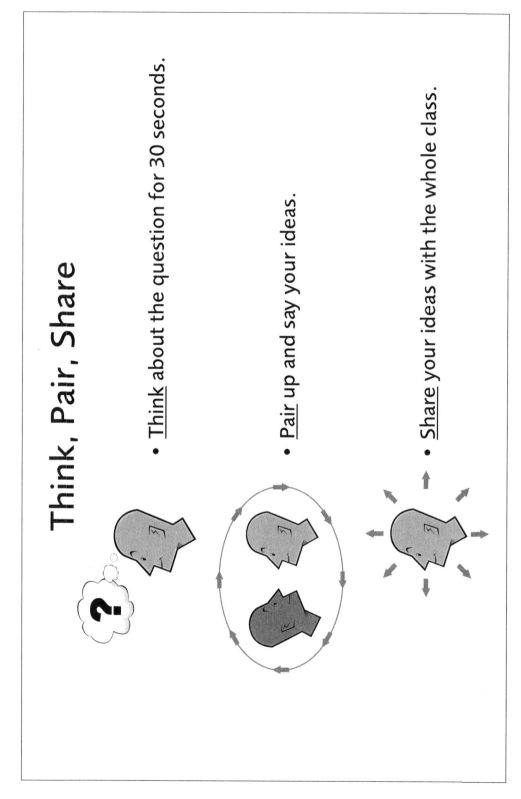

Think, Pair, Share

- Think about the question for 30 seconds.

- Pair up and say your ideas.

- Share your ideas with the whole class.

Routledge
Taylor & Francis Group

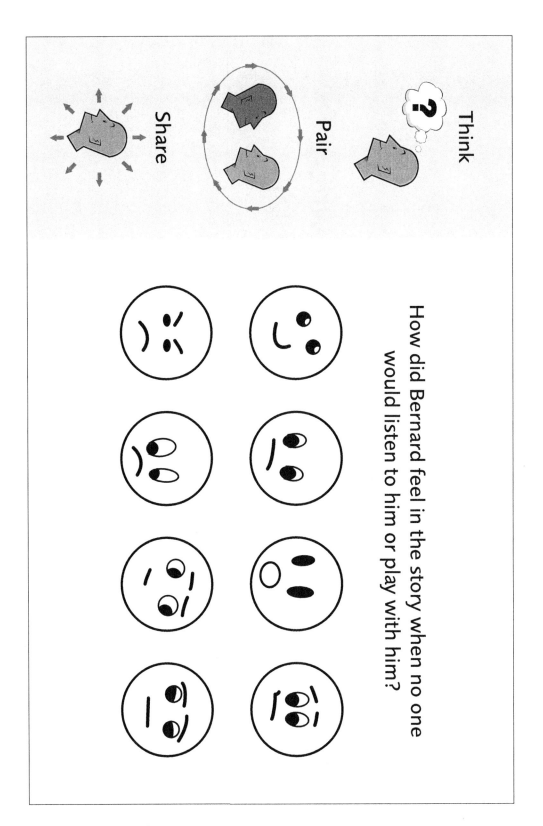

Think

Pair

Share

How did Bernard feel in the story when no one would listen to him or play with him?

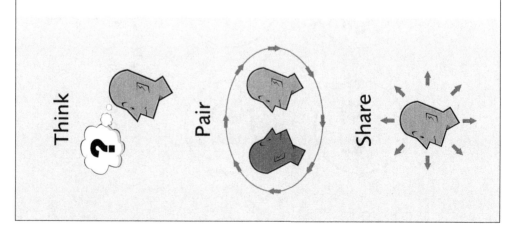

What happened when Bernard did not talk about his feelings?

Think

Pair

Share

Routledge
Taylor & Francis Group

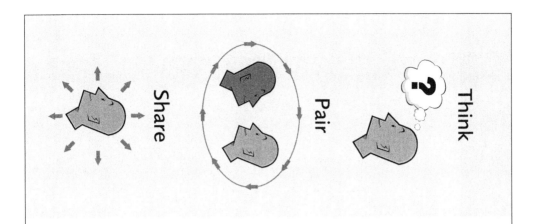

Think

Pair

Share

Did Bernard really get eaten by a monster or did he turn into the monster?

Routledge
Taylor & Francis Group

Session 5:

My body, thoughts and feelings all go together

Introduction to Session 5
My body, thoughts and feelings all go together

Young children may experience feelings as being things that come out of nowhere! We can teach them that often we have a thought which generates a feeling and then that feeling gets expressed in our bodies either internally, for example the feeling of butterflies in our tummies, or externally by the expression on our faces or how we are standing. In this way, we link the idea of thoughts, feelings and actions so that children can begin to become more conscious that thinking is related to feelings and actions.

This session provides opportunities for children to think and talk about how characters in pictures are feeling by looking at their faces and bodies, and then to guess what the character might be thinking.

Routledge
Taylor & Francis Group

Session 5: *My body, thoughts and feelings all go together*

Session objectives

- I will understand that my feelings and my thoughts can make my body change.

Key words

body, thinking, feelings, happy, sad, angry, excited, scared, surprised, bored, hurt

Session plan

Activity	Instructions	Resources
What are we doing?	• Put up relevant timetable cards so the children can easily see them. • Go through the timetable with the children so they know what will be happening to them during the session. • Take down each card at the completion of each activity.	'What are we doing?' cards
Agreement	• Revise the agreement and the importance of following it. • Put the agreement up where all children can see it.	Agreement template

The two main themes	• Show the children the themes poster which displays these phrases:
	  • **We all have the right to feel safe all of the time**
	  • **There is nothing so awful or small that we can't talk about it with someone**
	• Get the children to say the phrases out loud with you.
		Themes poster

Routledge
Taylor & Francis Group

Activity	Instructions	Resources
Review	• Read or watch *Not Now, Bernard*, focusing on the part when he turns into the monster. • Repeat a Think, Pair, Share activity with this question: 'What happened to Bernard's **body** when he did not talk about his feelings?'	*Not Now, Bernard* or watch at: www.youtube.com/watch?v=a2cjdRWmfdo 'Think, Pair, Share' slides
Why are we doing this?	• Go through the points on the 'Why are we doing this?' poster. • Ask the children if they have any questions.	'Why are we doing this?' poster 5
Key words	• Write the key words on the board for the children to see. • Get the children to say the words out loud with you and choose one of the following brief activities to help reinforce the new words. ◦ Break up the word into syllables. ◦ Say the first sound of the word. ◦ Put the word into a sentence. ◦ Practise explaining what the word means.	
Starting activity	• Sing the 'If You Know Your Body Parts' song.	Songs pack
Main activity 1	• Show the children a picture of someone smiling. • Ask the children how they think the person is feeling and how they know that they are feeling that way. • Show the children a picture of someone looking very sad. • Ask the children how they think the person is feeling and how they know that they are feeling that way. • Emphasise that we can see how people feel by what they are doing with their faces and sometimes their bodies.	Happy and sad feelings cards

Routledge
Taylor & Francis Group

Activity	Instructions	Resources
Main activity 2	• Show the children the picture of two children calling a boy names. • Use the story hand to ask the children questions about what is happening in this scene. • Ask the children how the characters might be feeling (give them a choice of two possible feelings if needed by using the feelings cards). • Ask the children how they know the characters are feeling this way. Focus on what their bodies are doing (e.g. faces, hands, body language). • Look at the handout 'What are the characters thinking?' Support the children to fill in thoughts in the thought bubble. • Conclude or summarise by telling the children our body does things to help us know how we are feeling.	Picture showing name calling Story hand What are the characters thinking? handout
End of lesson certificate	• Children complete the end of lesson certificate as a summary of what they have learnt today.	End of lesson certificate
Finishing activity as reward	• Refer to the reward chart and agreement. If the children have received 10 points, they can choose a game or song to finish with (e.g. repeat a game or song from the lesson or choose from the games or songs pack).	Games and songs packs

Everyday links to this session

• Focus throughout the week on this phrase from the themes poster:
  We all have the right to feel safe all the time.

• Sing 'If You Know Your Body Parts' again.

• Refer to recommended reading list for ideas about being scared.

Session 5: Resources

Why are we doing this session?

Session 5

This session will help us to...

- Know that our feelings and thoughts can make our bodies change.

Routledge
Taylor & Francis Group

Routledge
Taylor & Francis Group

What is she thinking?

Session 6:

Feeling safe

Introduction to Session 6
Feeling safe

This session is about reinforcing feelings and specifically looks at understanding the concept of safe and unsafe feelings.

In this session we explore the idea that sometimes feeling frightened can be fun and safe, for example going on a rollercoaster, and sometimes it is safe but not fun, for example going to the dentist can be pretty scary but it is also very important and a safe environment.

We also explore with children the idea that some things can make us feel happy or excited but aren't safe. For example, we might feel excited about a fight that is happening in the playground but it is not safe to be involved or to encourage it. You might be familiar with the dual concept of 'good' and 'bad' feelings and touches that sex education or protective behaviour programmes were based on in the past. It is much more realistic, and takes away the idea of fault or blame, to talk about 'safe' and 'unsafe' rather than good and bad.

For example, some children may feel excited by being touched on their sexual parts, even though it is not safe (or lawful) for them to be touched by adults in this way. It is possible that, at this point in the programme, a child reveals they have been touched in this way. So it is important to move away from the concept of good or bad and ensure the child understands that this is not a safe situation for them and it needs to be dealt with by an adult.

Aside from issues of abuse, there may be other types of experience, such as bullying or teasing, that children need to learn to be able to speak about and know that there is somewhere they can go if they are feeling unsafe. This is explored in Session 9 'Choosing my people network'.

Session 6: *Feeling safe*

Session objectives

- I will know that sometimes it is okay to feel scared.
- I will know that sometimes it is fun to feel scared.
- I will understand the difference between feeling scared and feeling unsafe.
- I will know that we all have the right to feel safe all of the time.

Key words

safe, unsafe, scared

Session plan

Activity	Instructions	Resources
What are we doing?	• Put up relevant timetable cards so the children can easily see them. • Go through the timetable with the children so they know what will be happening to them during the session. • Take down each card at the completion of each activity.	'What are we doing?' cards
Agreement	• Revise the agreement and the importance of following it. • Put the agreement up where all children can see it.	Agreement template and reward chart

The two main themes	• Show the children the themes poster which displays these phrases:
	  • **We all have the right to feel safe all of the time**
	  • **There is nothing so awful or small that we can't talk about it with someone**
	• Get the children to say the phrases out loud with you.
		Themes poster

Routledge
Taylor & Francis Group

Activity	Instructions	Resources
Review	• Get the children to do a Think, Pair, Share activity about something which happened to them this week that may have made them angry or sad.	'Think, Pair, Share' card
Why are we doing this?	• Go through the points on the 'Why are we doing this?' poster. • Ask the children if they have any questions.	'Why are we doing this?' poster 6

Key words	• Write the key words on the board for the children to see.
	• Get the children to say the words out loud with you and choose one of the following brief activities to help reinforce the new words.
	  ◦ Break up the word into syllables.
	  ◦ Say the first sound of the word.
	  ◦ Put the word into a sentence.
	  ◦ Practise explaining what the word means.	

Starting activity	• Sing the 'I Am a Tower of Strength' song.	Songs pack
Main activity	• Show the children the 'How safe am I?' and 'How do I feel?' scales. • Explain that safety goes from green, where you are safe, to orange, where you are becoming unsafe, and to red, where you are unsafe and in a dangerous situation. • Explain the feelings scale by saying that we can all have different feelings about different situations. There are no right or wrong feelings, just different feelings for different people. Some people might feel a little bit scared but still be having fun at the same time. Some people might feel quite scared but it is still fun. Then there are times when we feel really scared and it is not fun at all.	Scales for 'How safe am I?' and 'How do I feel?' (colour versions are included on the accompanying CD) Safety and feeling situation cards

Routledge
Taylor & Francis Group

Activity	Instructions	Resources
Main activity *(continued)*	• Demonstrate this idea by showing the children the example of the completed scales. There is a completed scale for 'going to the dentist', where the yellow star shows you may be feeling scared, that it's not fun at all but it's safe and important to go to the dentist. There are two completed examples for 'people calling me names' and a 'fight in the playground'. • Talk through each example with the children and ask them where they would put the star on the scales – emphasise again that we will all put the star in different places as we can all have different feelings about situations. • Show the children the other situation cards and get them to put stars on the scales. Discuss a few more situations and, where children mark the situation as unsafe, emphasise this would not be an okay situation and refer back to the themes poster: **We all have the right to feel safe all of the time.** • Let the children know that in the next lessons we will be learning about what to do when we feel unsafe.	
End of lesson certificate	• Children complete the end of lesson certificate as a summary of what they have learnt today.	End of lesson certificate
Finishing activity as reward	• Refer to the reward chart and agreement. If the children have received 10 points, they can choose a game or song to finish with (e.g. repeat a game or song from the lesson or choose from the games or songs pack).	Games and songs packs

Everyday links to this session

- Start and end the day by asking the children to name a time when they feel very safe (refer back to the situation cards if needed).

- Refer to feeling safe or unsafe when appropriate or relevant situations arise during the week.

- Sing 'I Am a Tower of Strength' again.

- Focus again this week on getting the children to use this phrase:
  We all have the right to feel safe all of the time.

Session 6: Resources

Why are we doing this session?

Session 6

This session will help us to...

- Know there are different types of scared feelings.

- Know we can all have different feelings sometimes.

- Know it is not okay to feel unsafe.

Think, Pair, Share

- <u>Think</u> about the question for 30 seconds.

- <u>Pair</u> up and say your ideas.

- <u>Share</u> your ideas with the whole class.

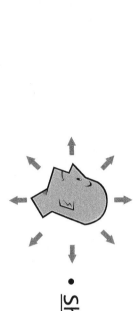

 Routledge
Taylor & Francis Group

Routledge
Taylor & Francis Group

This page may be photocopied for instructional use only. *First Steps to Safety programme*
© Carolyn Gelenter, Nadine Prescott and Belinda Riley 2014

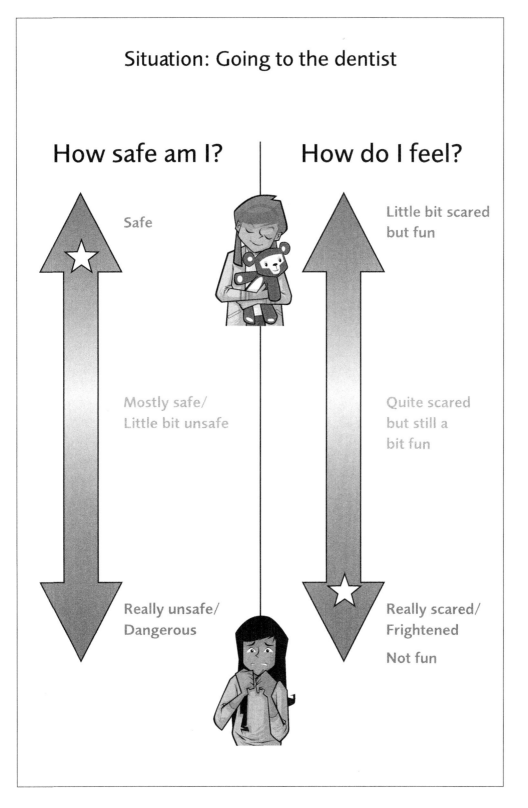

Situation: Going to the dentist

How safe am I?   ## How do I feel?

Safe

Little bit scared
but fun

Mostly safe/
Little bit unsafe

Quite scared
but still a
bit fun

Really unsafe/
Dangerous

Really scared/
Frightened

Not fun

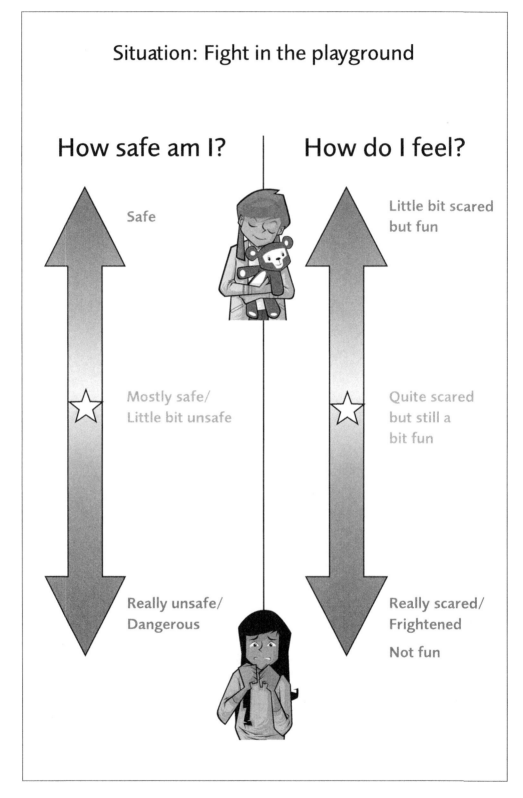

Situation: Fight in the playground

How safe am I?

Safe

Mostly safe/
Little bit unsafe

Really unsafe/
Dangerous

How do I feel?

Little bit scared
but fun

Quite scared
but still a
bit fun

Really scared/
Frightened

Not fun

Routledge
Taylor & Francis Group

Situation: People calling me names

How safe am I? | How do I feel?

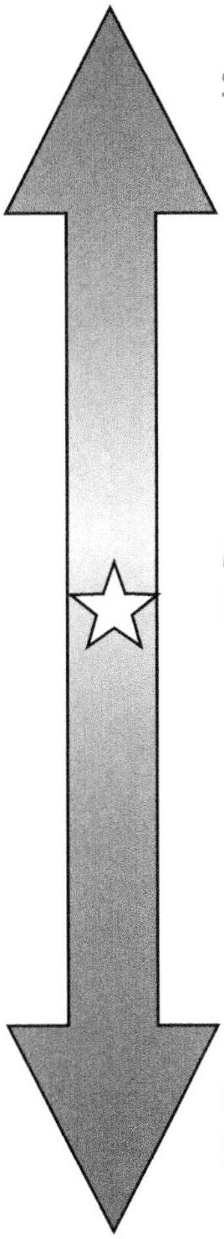

Safe

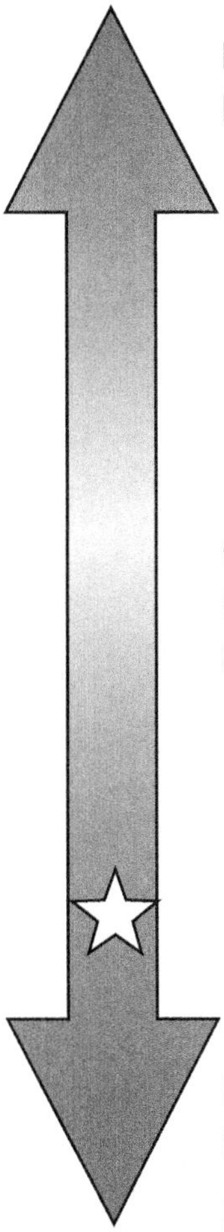

Little bit scared
but fun

Mostly safe/
Little bit unsafe

Quite scared
but still a
bit fun

Really unsafe/
Dangerous

Really scared/
Frightened

Not fun

Routledge
Taylor & Francis Group

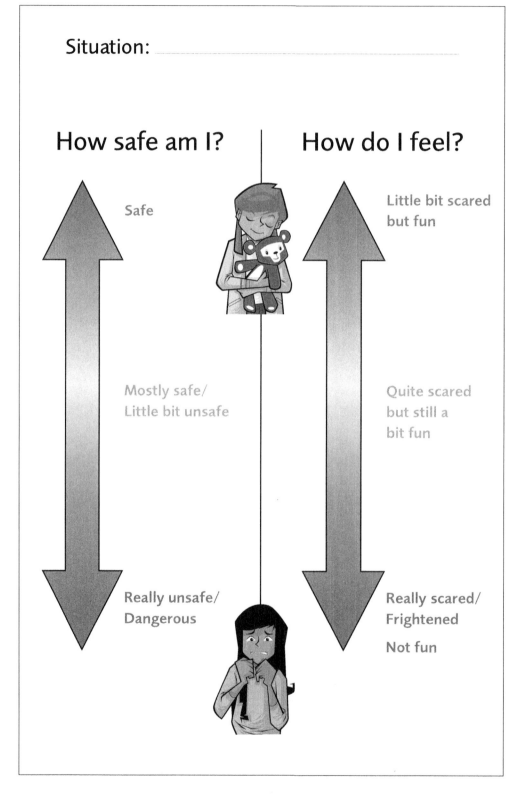

Situation: ....

How safe am I?   ## How do I feel?

Safe

Little bit scared
but fun

Mostly safe/
Little bit unsafe

Quite scared
but still a
bit fun

Really unsafe/
Dangerous

Really scared/
Frightened

Not fun

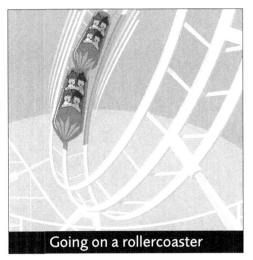

Going on a rollercoaster

Other children are laughing at me and calling me names

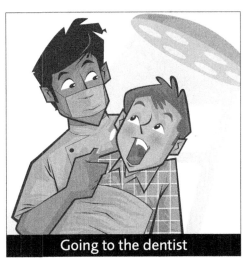

Going to the dentist

Going in a car without a seatbelt

Somebody shouting at me

It's my birthday party

I get lost in the shopping centre

There is a fight in the playground

Going on a plane

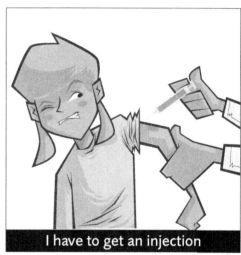

I have to get an injection

I have to read out loud in class

I get given an award at assembly

Session 7:

What my body does when I feel unsafe

Introduction to Session 7
What my body does when I feel unsafe

We all experience feelings in our bodies but it is only when we understand our bodies and have the vocabulary to express ourselves that we can begin to identify being scared (for example, that our knees shaking means we are scared).

The authors believe that it is possible to give children the age-appropriate vocabulary and awareness at a young age so that they can link what they think and feel to the way their body responds. The body, in turn, reinforces the feelings of being safe or unsafe, so it is important for children to understand what is happening in their body and to be able to respond to those feelings, even if they can't in the immediate situation.

We call the responses of our body 'early warning signs' and in this session we emphasise the importance of being aware of and taking note of those signs. Too often, children are taught to always look to others before they act, but we also need children to learn to trust their feelings and speak out for themselves if we are truly concerned as a society with keeping our children safe.

Session 7: *What my body does when I feel unsafe*

Session objectives

- I will know what my body does when it feels unsafe
- I will know what my 'early warning signs' are to feeling unsafe.
- I will know it is not okay to feel unsafe and we all have the right to feel safe all of the time.

Key words

'early warning signs'

Session plan

Activity	Instructions	Resources
What are we doing?	• Put up relevant timetable cards so the children can easily see them. • Go through the timetable with the children so they know what will be happening to them during the session. • Take down each card at the completion of each activity.	'What are we doing?' cards
Agreement	• Revise the agreement and the importance of following it. • Put the agreement up where all children can see it.	Agreement template and reward chart

The two main themes	• Show the children the themes poster which displays these phrases:
	  • **We all have the right to feel safe all of the time**
	  • **There is nothing so awful or small that we can't talk about it with someone**
	• Get the children to say the phrases out loud with you.
		Themes poster

Activity	Instructions	Resources
Review	• Refer back to the safe–unsafe scale. Ask two or three children to tell about a time when they felt very safe. • Use the story hand to help children structure their story.	Safe–unsafe scale Story hand
Why are we doing this?	• Go through the points on the 'Why are we doing this?' poster. • Ask the children if they have any questions.	'Why are we doing this?' poster 7
Key words	• Write the key words on the board for the children to see. • Get the children to say the words out loud with you and choose one of the following brief activities to help reinforce the new words. 　• Break up the word into syllables. 　• Say the first sound of the word. 　• Put the word into a sentence. 　• Practise explaining what the word means.	
Starting activity	• Play the 'Shake it' game (focus on those body parts that give us early warning signs).	Games pack
Main activity	**What our body does when it feels unsafe** • Choose some of the situations from Session 6 that the children identified as being associated with unsafe feelings. • Show the children the pictures of different body parts that tell us we feel unsafe. • Ask the children to think about what these body parts do when we feel unsafe, e.g. our knees might shake. • Write their responses on the picture for each body part to make them into posters to put up on the wall.	Safe–unsafe situation cards Pictures of body parts that give early warning signs

Activity	Instructions	Resources
	• Explain that the things our bodies do to tell us we are unsafe are called 'early warning signs'. This is how our bodies let us know we are not safe.	
End of lesson certificate	• Children complete the end of lesson certificate as a summary of what they have learnt today.	End of lesson certificate
Finishing activity as reward	• Refer to the reward chart and agreement. If the children have received 10 points, they can choose a game or song to finish with (e.g. repeat a game or song from the lesson or choose from the games or songs pack).	Games and songs packs

Everyday links to this session

• Get the children to repeat the words of the themes poster,
We all have the right to feel safe all of the time.

• Put the 'early warning signs' posters the children completed up on the classroom wall and refer to them as situations arise in the classroom during the week.

• Repeat the 'Shake it' game, focusing on those body parts that react as part of 'early warning signs'.

Session 7: Resources

Why are we doing this session?

Session 7

This session will help us to...

- Know what our bodies do when we are unsafe.

- Know what our 'early warning signs' are for feeling unsafe.

- Know it is *not* okay to feel unsafe.

Routledge
Taylor & Francis Group

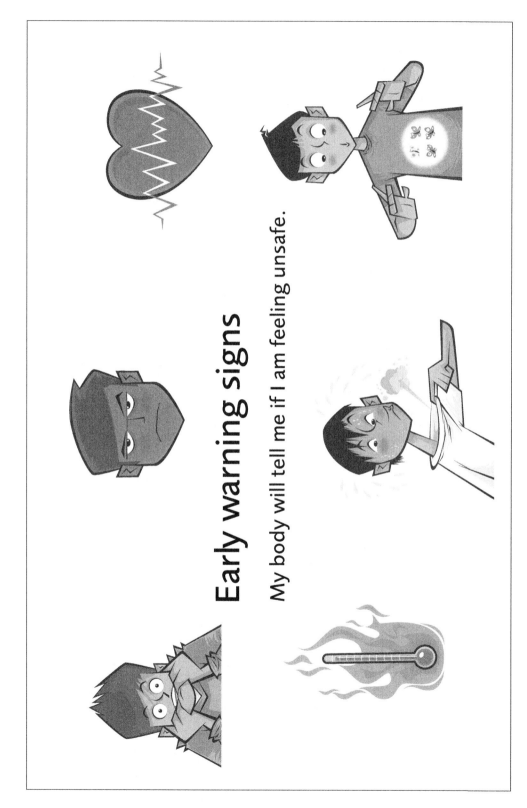

What does our heart do if we feel unsafe?

Write what our heart does if we feel unsafe in this box.

Routledge
Taylor & Francis Group

What does our stomach do if we feel unsafe?

Write what our stomach does if we feel unsafe in this box.

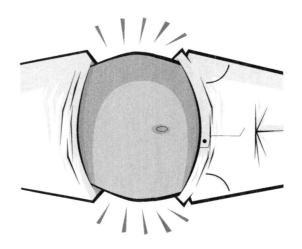

 Routledge
Taylor & Francis Group

What do our hands do if we feel unsafe?

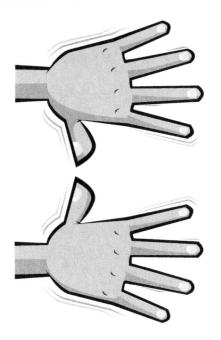

Write what our hands do if we feel unsafe in this box.

What does our face do if we feel unsafe?

Write what our face does if we feel unsafe in this box.

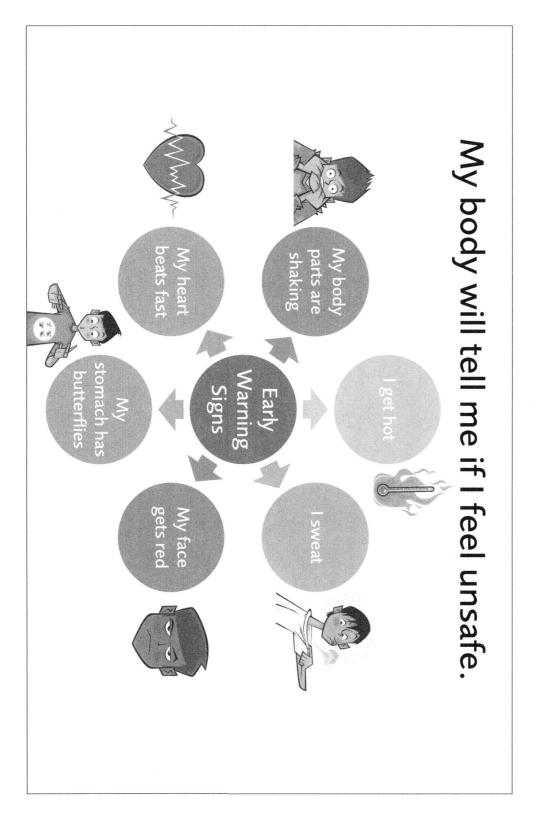

My body will tell me if I feel unsafe.

Routledge
Taylor & Francis Group

Session 8:

Behaviour choices

Introduction to Session 8
Behaviour choices

While sometimes it may feel as though we have no choices, especially as young people, and sometimes the choices facing us are not easy ones, all behaviours are indeed choices. Even very young children can be taught to make choices; for example, two-and three-year olds often make very determined choices about what they want to wear that day! Young children consistently make choices about what they want to play with, who they want to be friends with and what food they want to eat. Teaching children that they can choose to behave in certain ways is simply making the idea that we can make choices more conscious and concrete.

Sometimes children are in situations at school or home where they have little power to make choices. The authors are not advocating that children make choices about every aspect of their lives. As adults, caring for and educating children, we must take responsibility for them. However, not all adults behave in ways which keep the children's best interests at heart and, at these times, it is so important for young children to know that they do 'have a right to feel safe at all times'. If they are unable to exercise their choice not to be touched or teased at the time, they can still understand that they can make a choice to communicate about anything even if it is 'awful or a small thing'.

These behaviours are not something most children just learn; they need to be taught and reinforced in all sorts of situations in children's lives.

Routledge
Taylor & Francis Group

Session 8: *Behaviour choices*

Session objectives

- I will know that I can make a choice about how I behave.
- I will understand that every choice has a consequence.

Key words

choice, consequence, problem, solution

Session plan

Activity	Instructions	Resources
What are we doing?	• Put up relevant timetable cards so the children can easily see them. • Go through the timetable with the children so they know what will be happening to them during the session. • Take down each card at the completion of each activity.	'What are we doing?' cards
Agreement	• Revise the agreement and the importance of following it. • Put the agreement up where all children can see it.	Agreement template and reward chart

The two main themes	• Show the children the themes poster which displays these phrases:
	  • **We all have the right to feel safe all of the time**
	  • **There is nothing so awful or small that we can't talk about it with someone**
	• Get the children to say the phrases out loud with you.
		Themes poster

Review	• Review the children's 'Early warning signs' posters.	'Early warning signs' posters

Activity	Instructions	Resources
Why are we doing this?	• Go through the points on the 'Why are we doing this?' poster. • Ask the children if they have any questions.	'Why are we doing this?' poster 8
Key words	• Write the key words on the board for the children to see. • Get the children to say the words out loud with you and choose one of the following brief activities to help reinforce the new words. • Break up the word into syllables. • Say the first sound of the word. • Put the word into a sentence. • Practise explaining what the word means.	
Starting activity	Sing the 'It's All About Us' song.	Songs pack
Main activity	• Show the children the behaviour choice cards and ask them the questions on the cards. • For the question 'What could X do?', write down the children's responses. Choose two responses and talk about what the consequences of these responses would be. • Tell the children that there is a choice in how we behave and that each choice has a consequence. • Emphasise that we all have feelings. It is okay to have feelings but we need to make good behaviour choices about our feelings.	Behaviour choice cards
End of lesson certificate	• Children complete the end of lesson certificate as a summary of what they have learnt today.	End of lesson certificate

Activity	Instructions	Resources
Finishing activity as reward	• Refer to the reward chart and agreement. If the children have received 10 points, they can choose a game or song to finish with (e.g. repeat a game or song from the lesson or choose from the games or songs pack).	Games and songs packs

Everyday links to this session

- Get the children to repeat the two phrases on the themes poster.

- Sing 'It's All About Us' again.

- When there is an opportunity in the week to air a problem, such as a difficulty in the playground, get the children to brainstorm different ways of solving the problem. Remind them that there is always a choice.

- Set up a problem-solving activity in a PE class where the children have to work together to find a way to cross a space.

Routledge
Taylor & Francis Group

Session 8: Resources

Why are we doing this session?

Session 8

This session will help us to...

- Know we can make choices about how we behave.

- Understand that every choice we make has a consequence.

Behaviour choice

- What is the girl doing?
- What is the girl thinking?
- Is the girl safe?
- What could the girl have done instead?

Routledge
Taylor & Francis Group

This page may be photocopied for instructional use only. *First Steps to Safety programme*
© Carolyn Gelenter, Nadine Prescott and Belinda Riley 2014

Behaviour choice

- The boy has forgotten what his homework is.

- How does he feel?

- What is he thinking?

- What could the boy do?

Behaviour choice

- What are the boys doing?
- How do the boys feel?
- What are the boys thinking?
- What could the boys do?

Behaviour choice

- What is the boy doing?
- How does the boy feel?
- What is the boy thinking?
- What could the boy do?

Routledge
Taylor & Francis Group

Session 9:

Choosing my people network

Introduction to Session 9
Choosing my people network

While children can and should be encouraged to make choices, they are often not in a position to act on those choices. For example, it is difficult for children to remove themselves physically from a situation where they are being abused by an adult. This is why it is so important for children to understand they can make a choice about telling a responsible adult who is able to do something about the situation.

Children also need to understand the difference between problems that may need adult intervention and problems that they can learn to solve themselves. We do not want children running to adults for every problem that arises in their day! The understanding of what feeling safe and unsafe feels like in their bodies can help children make the decision about whether to consult an adult or not.

This session reinforces the concept of safety in choosing people who the child feels safe with, and can act on their behalf. At the end of this session, children should have a list of people they can turn to in their people network.

Routledge
Taylor & Francis Group

Session 9:
Choosing my people network

Session objectives

- I will know who to go to for help if I don't feel safe.
- I will know what 'my people network' means.

Key words

people network, asking for help

Session plan		
Activity	**Instructions**	**Resources**
What are we doing?	• Put up relevant timetable cards so the children can easily see them. • Go through the timetable with the children so they know what will be happening to them during the session. • Take down each card at the completion of each activity.	'What are we doing?' cards
Agreement	• Revise the agreement and the importance of following it. • Put the agreement up where all children can see it. • Revise the points and rewards.	Agreement template and reward chart

The two main themes	• Show the children the themes poster which displays these phrases:
	  • **We all have the right to feel safe all of the time**
	  • **There is nothing so awful or small that we can't talk about it with someone**
	• Get the children to say the phrases out loud with you.
		Themes poster

Activity	Instructions	Resources
Review	• Ask the children whether they had any problems they needed to solve this week and how they managed to solve them.	
Why are we doing this?	• Go through the points on the 'Why are we doing this?' poster. • Ask the children if they have any questions.	'Why are we doing this?' poster 9
Key words	• Write the key words on the board for the children to see. • Get the children to say the words out loud with you and choose one of the following brief activities to help reinforce the new words. 　　◦ Break up the word into syllables. 　　◦ Say the first sound of the word. 　　◦ Put the word into a sentence. 　　◦ Practise explaining what the word means.	
Starting activity	• Sing the 'HELP' song.	Songs pack
Main activity	**My people network** • Explain to the children that we need lots of different people in our life who we can go to if we need help to feel safe. This will be our 'people network' of people who can help us when we need it. • We are going to think about what sort of things would make someone good at giving us help. • Draw a line down the middle of a whiteboard or a flip-chart page. On one side, draw a smiley face and on the other side, draw a sad face. • Hold up each of the qualities cards one at a time (the cards that list different qualities people can have). • Ask the children to say whether this would be a good thing for a helping person in our network to be or not.	Whiteboard or flip chart, quality cards and 'My people network' worksheet

Activity	Instructions	Resources
Main activity *(continued)*	• Stick the labels under the happy or sad face. • Ask the children to think about some people they know who have lots of the qualities under the smiley face. • Ask the children to complete the 'My people network' worksheet (where they have to draw four people who they want to be in their 'people network'). • Choose two or three children to show the rest of the class their 'My people network' worksheet and tell about who is in their network.	
End of lesson certificate	• Children complete the end of lesson certificate as a summary of what they have learnt today.	End of lesson certificate
Finishing activity as reward	• Refer to the reward chart and agreement. If the children have received 10 points, they can choose a game or song to finish with (e.g. repeat a game or song from the lesson or choose from the games or songs pack).	Games and songs packs

Everyday links to this session

• Start to focus more on the second phrase on the themes poster: **There is nothing so awful or small that we can't talk about it with someone.**
• Stick the children's 'My people network' worksheets up on the classroom wall.
• Leave the qualities cards out for the children to refer back to.
• Throughout the week, see whether the children can think of any more people to join their network.
• Ask an adult chosen to be in a 'network' to visit the classroom. Get the children to explain why this person was chosen.
• If you see an adult from a child's network in the school, point them out to the children.
• Praise children throughout the week for showing the qualities placed under the smiley face.
• Sing the 'HELP' song again.

Session 9: Resources

Why are we doing this session?

Session 9

This session will help us to...

- Know who to go to for help.
- Know what a 'people network' is.

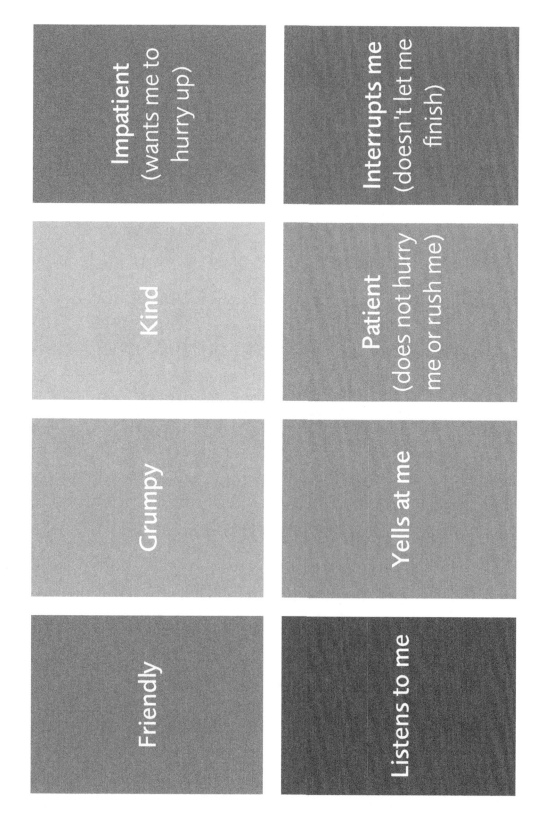

Impatient (wants me to hurry up)

Interrupts me (doesn't let me finish)

Kind

Patient (does not hurry me or rush me)

Grumpy

Yells at me

Friendly

Listens to me

My people network

Name _____

- My people network is the people I can go to for help.

- Here is a picture of the people in my network.

 Routledge
Taylor & Francis Group

Session 10:

Asking for help

Introduction to Session 10
Asking for help

We have included this session as a way of teaching children how they can go about asking for help. While we are encouraging children throughout these sessions that they can communicate about anything even if it is 'awful or small', the authors also recognise from our combined experiences, and working with children in early years, schools, therapy services and social services, that not all children have the skills, knowledge or confidence to be able to ask for help.

This session reinforces the two main protective behaviours themes by explicitly teaching children – through role play and games – how they can go about asking help from adults.

Routledge
Taylor & Francis Group

Session 10: *Asking for help*

Session objectives

- I will know how to ask 'my people network' for help if I feel unsafe.
- I will know there is nothing so awful or small that we can't talk about it.

Key words

asking for help, people network

Session plan

Activity	Instructions	Resources
What are we doing?	• Put up relevant timetable cards so the children can easily see them. • Go through the timetable with the children so they know what will be happening to them during the session. • Take down each card at the completion of each activity.	'What are we doing?' cards
Agreement	• Revise the agreement and the importance of following it. • Put the agreement up where all children can see it.	Agreement template and reward chart

The two main themes	• Show the children the themes poster which displays these phrases:
	  • **We all have the right to feel safe all of the time**
	  • **There is nothing so awful or small that we can't talk about it with someone**
	• Get the children to say the phrases out loud with you.
		Themes poster

Routledge
Taylor & Francis Group

Activity	Instructions	Resources
Review	• Ask two children to show the class their 'My people network' worksheets from the last lesson. • Remind the children that a 'people network' is a group of people we can go to for help.	'My people network' worksheets from last lesson
Why are we doing this?	• Go through the points on the 'Why are we doing this?' poster. • Ask the children if they have any questions.	'Why are we doing this?' poster 10

Key words	• Write the key words on the board for the children to see.
	• Get the children to say the words out loud with you and choose one of the following brief activities to help reinforce the new words.
	  ◦ Break up the word into syllables.
	  ◦ Say the first sound of the word.
	  ◦ Put the word into a sentence.
	  ◦ Practise explaining what the word means.	

Starting activity	• Play the 'Help be my eyes' game.	Games pack
Main activity	• Ask the children to think of some times when they might not feel safe and may need help. • Use the help situation cards to help the children think of ideas if needed. • Show the children the 'How to ask for help' card. • Choose one of the situations generated by the children and practise asking for help in this situation using the 'How to ask for help' card.	Help situation cards 'How to ask for help' card
End of lesson certificate	• Children complete the end of lesson certificate as a summary of what they have learnt today.	End of lesson certificate

Activity	Instructions	Resources
Finishing activity as reward	• Refer to the reward chart and agreement. If the children have received 10 points, they can choose a game or song to finish with (e.g. repeat a game or song from the lesson or choose from the games or songs pack).	Games and songs packs

Everyday links to this session

• Throughout the week, get the children to focus on saying the second phrase from the themes poster: **There is nothing so awful or small that we can't talk about it with someone.**

• Stick the 'How to ask for help' card on the wall in the classroom.

• Sing the 'HELP' song again.

• Specifically point out during the week times when children are helping someone else.

You can now give children their end of programme certificates.

Session 10: Resources

Why are we doing this session?

Session 10

This session will help us to...

- Know how to ask our 'people network' for help.

How to ask for help

- Choose one of your network people.

- Say to your network person: 'Excuse me, I need your help please. It's about feeling safe.'

- Tell your network person what has happened.

- If they cannot help you, tell another network person.

Routledge
Taylor & Francis Group

Help card

- You feel scared walking to school.

Help card

- Someone keeps calling you names all the time.

Routledge
Taylor & Francis Group

Help card

- You had an argument with someone.

Help card

- You feel worried about something that happened at home.

Conclusion: where to from here?

You have now completed all of the sessions of the First Steps to Safety programme. We hope that you enjoyed it and that your children are feeling empowered to keep themselves safe!

While the programme is now complete, it is important to keep reinforcing the principles of protective behaviours. We recommend that you take the following actions to ensure your children continue to feel confident about managing their own safety.

- Read further related stories (see the recommended reading list).
- Refer back to key words and strategies as everyday situations arise.
- Generally use the key words throughout the school day.
- Arrange regular visits from the children's people network.
- Keep the posters and children's work displayed.
- Hold revision sessions at whole school assemblies.
- Continue to sing the songs from the programme.
- Get some older children to present some of their work at an assembly or to another class.
- Invite parents in for a follow-up session – get some children to present the key points they have learned.
- Set some related homework once a week using the lesson topics and activities to get children to talk to their parents or carers about keeping safe.
- Send home a key word bank.
- Send home the posters from the programme.
- Take photos during the activities and display them in the classroom.

We all have the right to feel safe all of the time

There is nothing so awful or small that we can't talk about it with someone

What to do if you are worried a child is at risk or is being abused

Everyone who comes into contact with children and families in their everyday work, including those practitioners who do not have a specific role in safeguarding children, have a duty to safeguard and promote the welfare of children.

All children have the right to be safe and to be protected. So, it is important that you seek help if:

- A child tells you about something that has upset or harmed them, or something that has happened to another child.

- A child shows signs of physical injury for which there appears to be no satisfactory explanation or is accompanied by an allegation of abuse.

- A child's behaviour indicates or suggests that he or she is being abused.

- You witness worrying behaviour from one child to another.

- You observe worrying behaviour or attitudes by another worker towards a child that makes you feel uncomfortable in some way.

It is also important that you are familiar with your organisation's safeguarding and child protection policy; in particular, the names of your designated lead for Safeguarding and how to contact them.

If you are worried that a child is being abused or a child has disclosed something to you that is causing you concern, there is a list below of what you should and should not do (see also HM Government, 2006).

DO'S

- Do listen.

- Do reflect and summarise what the child is saying to check you are following.

- If appropriate, do ask open questions.

- Do take what the child is saying seriously and reassure the child that they did the right thing to tell you.

- Do make a written account of your conversation and observations, using the child's own words.

- Do ascertain the child's wishes and feelings.

- Do date your notes and record the time and place where disclosure happened.

- Do follow the procedures of your safeguarding policy.

DON'TS

- Don't show disbelief, anger or revulsion.

- Don't attempt to explain the actions of other people, e.g. by saying 'I can't imagine your mum doing that'.

- Don't promise confidentiality.

- Don't ask leading questions, such as 'Was it your mum who did this?', 'Has your brother been thumping you again?', 'Are you sure it was your father who caused those bruises?' Don't ask leading questions as you could contaminate evidence in a criminal investigation.

- Don't investigate as you may jeopardise a criminal investigation.

Always record your concerns or the information you gathered, including details of decisions taken about next steps, and about whether to share this information or not.

You may also contact:

- Your local authority's children's social care department

- NSPCC – tel. 0808 800 5000

- Police

- ChildLine – tel. 0800 1111

General resources
(needed for all sessions)

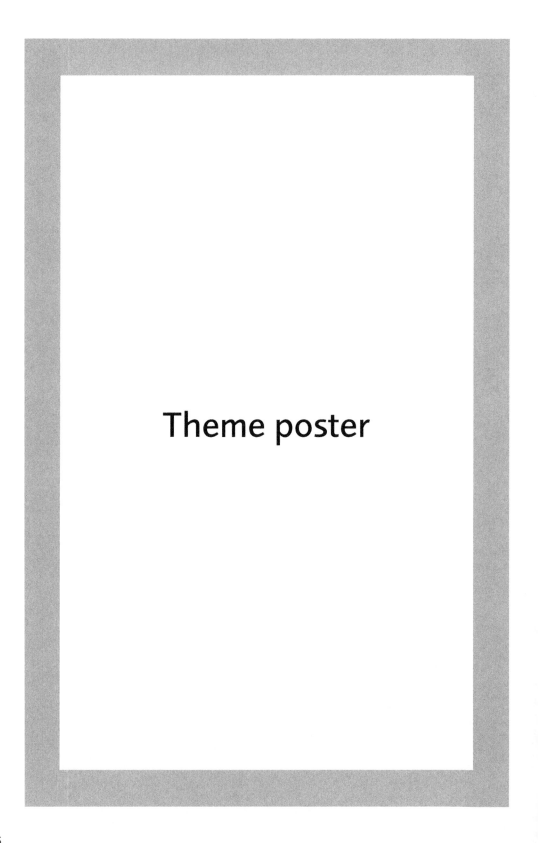

Theme poster

First Steps to Safety

There is nothing so awful or small that we can't talk about it with someone.

We all have the right to feel safe all of the time.

'What are we doing today?' timetable cards

What are we doing today?

First Steps to Safety

The two important things to remember about being safe

There is nothing so awful or small that we can't talk about it with someone.

We all have the right to feel safe all of the time.

Routledge
Taylor & Francis Group

Starter

Routledge
Taylor & Francis Group

Why are we doing this?

Review

Key words

shout
light streets dark
running
one gorgeous
great
drink slowly
group Lovely
like

Song

Routledge
Taylor & Francis Group

Activity

Routledge
Taylor & Francis Group

Learning break

Routledge
Taylor & Francis Group

Finishing activity

Games pack

Hide the teddy

- Sit the children in a circle.

- One child is asked to leave the room.

- Another child hides a teddy or another object somewhere that is not too obvious but not too easy to find.

- Once the teddy is hidden, the child outside comes back in.

- All of the children clap to help that child find the teddy.

- The closer the child is, the louder the clapping becomes.

Monsters

- Put the children into a circle, sitting on chairs if possible.

- One child is chosen to be a 'monster'.

- That child approaches the other children, acting like a 'monster'.

- When a child is approached, they must quickly call out the name of another child or they turn into a monster.

- When the name of another child is called, the monster must turn to that child and approach them.

- That child then calls out the name of another child before the monster reaches them.

- If the monster catches another child, they then become the monster.

Compliment circle

- Put the children into a circle, sitting on chairs.

- Ask one child to approach another child they think has been following the class agreement well.

- Get the first child to tell the second child what they did well.

- Encourage the children to talk directly to each other.

- It may be useful for the teacher to start off the activity by giving a model.

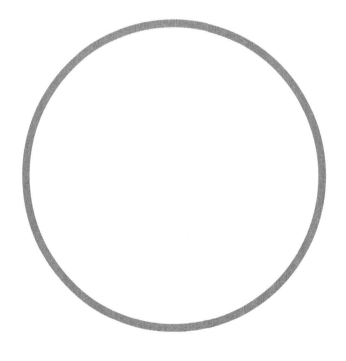

Help be my eyes

- Get the children to sit in a large circle.

- Place some small objects on the floor (e.g. a small bean bag, a pencil, a ruler).

- Blindfold one child or ask child to close their eyes.

- Choose another child to be their eyes and lead them to the other side of the circle, so they don't walk on any of the objects.

Routledge
Taylor & Francis Group

Shake it!

- Get the children to stand up.

- Give the children instructions to shake a certain body part, e.g. shake your arm, shake your leg, shake your fingers, shake your thumb, shake your tongue, shake your elbow.

- The children can only shake if you say 'Shake your ...' in your instruction.

- If you just say the body part, e.g. arm, leg, finger, the children cannot move.

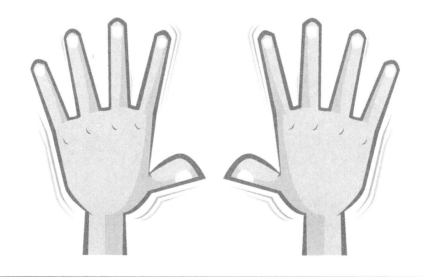

Routledge
Taylor & Francis Group

Pass the smile

- The teacher chooses a person to start.
- The first person chooses another person.
- Look towards them and smile!
- If you get smiled at, pass it on!

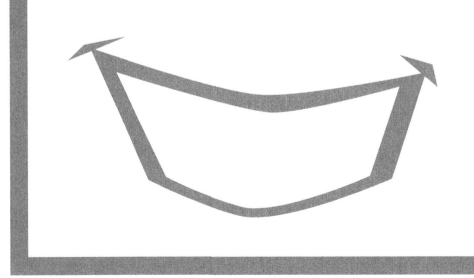

Songs pack

The Hokey Cokey

You put your right arm in
You put your right arm out
In out, in out, shake it all about
You do the hokey cokey and you turn around
That's how we learn about us.

Verse 2: repeat for left arm
Verse 3: repeat for right leg
Verse 4: repeat for left leg
Verse 5: repeat with whole body

(Can also introduce any other body part)

Routledge
Taylor & Francis Group

Head and Shoulders, Knees and Toes

Head, shoulders, Knees and toes, Knees and toes,
These are parts of us that grow, Parts that grow -ow -ow-ow,
Along with all our bo-o-o-o-dy, We are going to learn a lot about,
A lot about!

Body parts we need to know, Need to know
Arms and legs and mouth and nose, Mouth and no-o-o-ose,
In the cold we need to keep them warm, And try to keep ourselves
from harm, Any harm.

We are going to learn about ourselves, About ourselves,
How we feel and think and act, And to make some choices,
We can learn to keep ourselves safe, And to choose how we
behave, How we behave!

Then repeat verse 1 to end of song.

I Am a Tower of Strength

I am a tower of strength within and without
I am a tower of strength within [repeat]
Oh fear, slip away, slip away
Oh fear, slip from my heart
Oh fear, slip away, slip away
Oh fear, slip from my heart

Routledge
Taylor & Francis Group

It's All About Us

(sung to the tune of 'Today's Monday')

Today's important, today's important
Today we learn about ourselves
Is everybody ready?*
It's all about us!

(* Can change to 'Today we learn about feeling safe, our bodies')

R Routledge
Taylor & Francis Group

If You Know Your Body Parts

(sung to the tune of 'If You're Happy and You Know It')

If you know your body parts
Say yes
Say YES
If you know your body parts
Say yes
Say YES
If you know the names of parts
And you know what's in your heart
Then you can learn to tell others how you feel
I feel good!

If you know how you feel
Say I do
Say I DO
If you know you feel
Say I do
Say I DO
If you know how you feel
Then you can make a deal
To only do what makes you feel right
I feel right!

If you know right from wrong
Say right
Say RIGHT
If you know right from wrong
Say right
Say RIGHT
If you know right from wrong
Then you can sing this song
And learn how to say no if you need
Say NO!

Routledge
Taylor & Francis Group

HELP!

H ... E ...L ... P (said as letters)
Sound it out
With an H and an E and an L and a P
HELP
Starts with a 'huh' (said as the sound) and ends with a 'puh' (sound)
H ... E ...L ... P (said as letters)
HELP!

H ... E ...L ... P
Who needs help? (teacher says)
With an H and an E and an L and a P
We all need help (children say)
Starts with a 'huh' and ends with a 'puh'
H ... E ...L ... P
HELP!

H ... E ...L ... P
Where do we go?
With an H and E and an L and a P
To people we know
Starts with a 'huh' and ends with a 'puh'
H ... E ...L ... P
HELP!

H ... E ...L ... P
Sometimes we give it
With an H and an E and an L and a P
Sometimes we need it
Starts with a 'huh' and ends with a 'puh'
H ... E ...L ... P
HELP!

Routledge
Taylor & Francis Group

Recommended reading list

- *Not Now, Bernard* (1980) by David McKee or see www.youtube.com/watch?v=a2CjdRWmfdo

- *The Elephant and the Bad Baby* (1973) by Elfrida Vipoint and illustrated by Raymond Briggs

- *Mr Gumpy's Outing* by John Burningham

- *The Rainbow Fish* by Marcus Pfister

- *Dr Dog* (1994) by Babette Cole

- *The Piggy Book* (1996) by Anthony Browne

- *The Tunnel* (1997) by Anthony Browne

- *John Brown Rose and the Midnight Cat* (1980) by Jenny Wagner and illustrated by Ron Brooks

- *Two Monsters* (1980) by David McKee

- *Charlie and Lola* books by Lauren Child

- *We're Going on a Bear Hunt* (20 year anniversary edition 2009) by Michael Rosen and illustrated by Helen Oxenbury

- *A Dark Dark Tale* (2004) by Ruth Brown

Class agreement and reward chart

Class Agreement

First Steps to Safety

Our rules for First Steps to Safety lessons:

1 ....

2 ....

3 ....

4 ....

Write your name here to say you agree:

....

....

....

....

....

Agreement

....

Routledge
Taylor & Francis Group

Reward chart

First Steps to Safety

Our agreements (Put in agreements in this column)	Our points (Put tally points in this column)

Routledge
Taylor & Francis Group

Certificates

End of lesson certificate

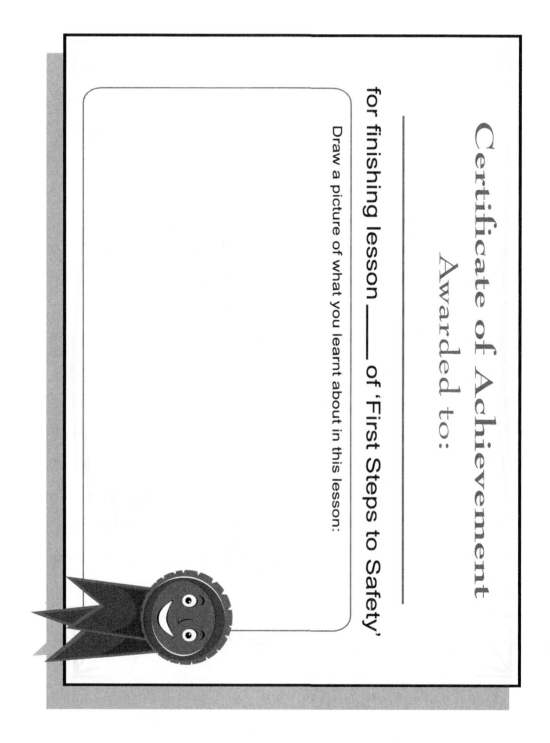

Certificate of Achievement

Awarded to:

_____

for finishing lesson ____ of 'First Steps to Safety'

_____

Draw a picture of what you learnt about in this lesson:

Routledge
Taylor & Francis Group

End of programme certificate

This Certificate is awarded to:

....

For finishing all of the lessons in

First Steps to Safety

Signed: ....

Date: ....

Story hand and 'Take a Word for a Walk' strategy sheets

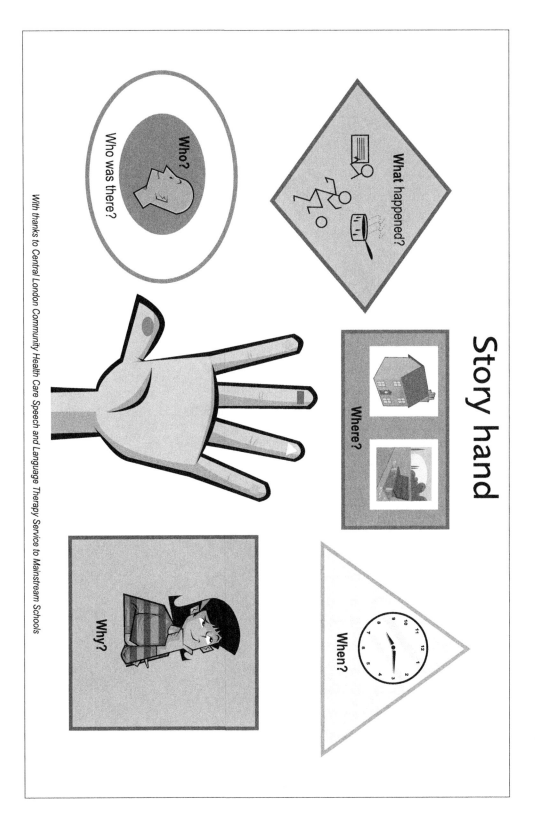

Story hand

Who?
Who was there?

What happened?

Where?

Why?

When?

With thanks to Central London Community Health Care Speech and Language Therapy Service to Mainstream Schools

Routledge
Taylor & Francis Group

Take a Word for a Walk

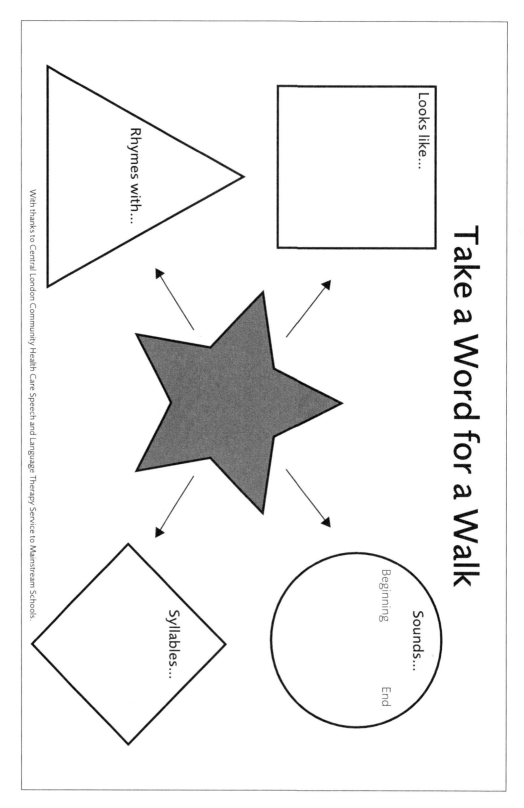

Looks like...

Rhymes with...

Sounds...

Beginning   End

Syllables...

With thanks to Central London Community Health Care Speech and Language Therapy Service to Mainstream Schools.

Routledge
Taylor & Francis Group

Sun and cloud cards

Sun

Cloud

Routledge
Taylor & Francis Group

Feelings cards

Happy

Sad

Angry

Excited

Scared

Surprised

Bored

Hurt

Routledge
Taylor & Francis Group

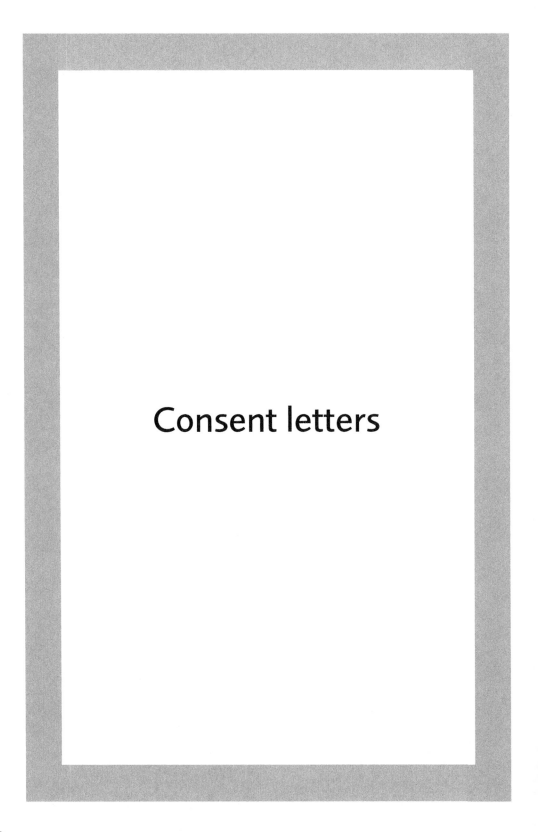

Consent letters

Consent letter for parents or carers

Dear <Name of Parent/Carer>

As part of our school's ongoing commitment to prioritising safeguarding <Name of School> is implementing a new safety programme for children aged 4–7 years which focuses on empowering children around personal safety. The programme is based on a Protective Behaviours programme, focusing around two main themes 'We all have the right to feel safe all of the time' and 'There is nothing so awful or small that we can't talk about it with someone'. The information provided to children is generic and can be applied to a range of situations that may arise for them, such as bullying, internet safety, being harmed, feeling sad or feeling unsafe.

Schools have a statutory responsibility to ensure that children are safe and their welfare is promoted. They are required to educate children as part of the curriculum around safety issues. <Name of School> takes safeguarding extremely seriously and recognises the importance of ensuring that children have an awareness of and strategies for keeping safe and have identified the First Steps of Safety programme to provide this.

The First Steps to Safety programme's overall aims and objectives are outlined below.

Overall aims

- To empower children to feel safe and know they have a right to feel safe.
- To give children the confidence and ability to assertively manage their own safety.
- To give children the skills to take responsibility for their own bodies, thoughts, feelings and behaviour.
- To enable children with a range of communication abilities to ask for help.

The programme is designed to be taught over 10 sessions, using a variety of activities, including songs and games to introduce and reinforce the themes.

We are sending you this letter to inform you of the programme and to ask your permission for your child to participate in the programme. An information evening for parents has also been arranged on the <insert date> which you are very welcome to attend.

If you would like further information on the programme, please contact <insert name>.

Yours sincerely

<insert name>Head Teacher
<Name of School>

Consent letter

PARTICIPATION IN THE FIRST STEPS TO SAFETY PROGRAMME

I consent to my child ....

(full name of child please) participating in the First Steps to Safety programme.

Signature: ....

Name: ....

Date: ....

Routledge
Taylor & Francis Group

References

- HM Government (2006) *What To Do if You're Worried a Child is Being Abused*, London: HMSO. Available online at: www.gov.uk/government/publications/what-to-do-if-youre-worried-a-child-is-being-abused

- Radford L et al. (2011) *Child Abuse and Neglect in the UK Today*. Available online at: www.nspcc.org.uk/inform/research/findings/child_abuse_neglect_research_PDF_wdf84181.pdf

- Sullivan PM, Knutson JF (2000) Maltreatment and disabilities: a population-based epidemiological study. *Child Abuse and Neglect*. 24(10): 1257–73.

Printed in Great Britain
by Amazon

20171465R00106